David Gregory has written a book that is sure to help many people no matter where they are on their spiritual journey. He authentically shares his personal story of recovery in a way that provides insight into "the spiritual approach" to both the challenges and the joys of life. His natural wit and humor shine through even the darkest moments of his life providing candor and insight. After reading this book, each reader will come away with some useful gem for living life to the fullest!

Rev. Paul Hasselbeck D.D.S.
Unity Village Kansas

"If you have wanted to learn how to stay in the "now" – in the present moment; If you have wanted to learn to trust the unfolding of each day and each life event; If you have wanted to change your life by changing your thoughts…….then this book is for you! Show up to your life in a way that leaves you feeling joy-full, peace-full, and hope-full. You'll love that David Gregory has shared his own story in a way that will touch your heart, your soul, and your funny-bone.

Linda Beushausen RN PhD CHPCA,
President and CEO Hospice at Home, Inc.
President and CEO Hospice at Home
VP Life Transitions and Advance
Healthcare Planning Lakeland HealthCare

The author has been there and back so many times and has risen from those ashes to live a fully vibrant life. He is the real deal. This is relatable spirituality, spoken with personal honesty. It is at once funny and poignant. Show up for this book. It could nudge you into your next big thing and change your life.

Joan Wendland, Author of:
Lets Fall In Love On Wednesday

JUST
SHOW
UP

Ya Gotta Do It Anyway

DAVID STANLEY GREGORY

iUniverse®

JUST SHOW UP
YA GOTTA DO IT ANYWAY

iUniverse books may be ordered through booksellers or by contacting:

iUniverse
1663 Liberty Drive
Bloomington, IN 47403
www.iuniverse.com
844-349-9409

Because of the dynamic nature of the Internet, any web addresses or links contained in this book may have changed since publication and may no longer be valid. The views expressed in this work are solely those of the author and do not necessarily reflect the views of the publisher, and the publisher hereby disclaims any responsibility for them.

Any people depicted in stock imagery provided by Getty Images are models, and such images are being used for illustrative purposes only.
Certain stock imagery © Getty Images.

ISBN: 978-1-4917-2598-6 (sc)
ISBN: 978-1-4917-2599-3 (e)

Library of Congress Control Number: 2014904029

Print information available on the last page.

iUniverse rev. date: 11/02/2023

Contents

Introduction

Life is full of change, and if we forget what we know, we struggle with outcomes. We all forget what we have learned. We all forget what we have studied. We forget what we know in the midst of crisis or love. This is when we need to be still. This is when I learned that I was to remember and nudge myself and others into the truth that lives within. I wrote this book in the realization that I had overcome sexual abuse, alcoholism, depression, my sexual orientation, and a religious practice that was judgmental and limiting. I wrote this book because of the sudden loss of my brother and mentally ill father who committed suicide. It was the next right thing for me to do. I finally loved myself enough to tell you that if my message can give you the hope, the faith, and the courage to address anything, you will be set free. And if you already have addressed major happenings in your life, then this is the book of nudges. You may hear something stir in your soul that reminds you of what you have already tackled. It will be the voice of God that lives within that gives you the right to once again let it go, only quickly this time. My life is still very much in progress. Even though I decided to do the big things that I came here to do, I will now have the tools to finesse and tweak the time I have left in this life. We are *one* in this life, and my experience is to give away the gifts I have recognized, so that I may keep them. It's your turn to hear what you need to hear. I compassionately stand next to you in loving consciousness as you embrace whatever you need to embrace to give you the freedom that has been guaranteed to us all. So take what you need and leave the rest. And please remember, it is rightfully yours for the taking.

So how many degrees or credentials does David Stanley Gregory have, in order to profess this wisdom you are about to read?

Credentials

I, David Stanley Gregory, solemnly swear the following is the truth, the whole truth, and nothing but the truth. You will find no 'doctor' in front of my name, no physiotherapist in my title, and no master's degree on the inside cover. However, you will find a man who has experienced what it takes to have a master's degree in life. And please note that David Gregory is currently working on his doctorate in how to keep doing what he is doing in the present moment. He is committed to continuing this line of study for as long as he is on the planet.

Those of you who have not had or completed a formal education, please take note: you can find yourself in the company of the Buddha and the Christ and many other great sages of old. They had no formal education but were still considered fully educated masters. I have had the privilege of being opened to new information by an array of great teachers. Truly the teacher and the student are on common ground.

Education

High School: I did poorly, but graduated while living on my own.

College: I went directly after high school but could not financially afford to stay. At age forty-two, and in recovery for alcoholism, I went back to school and attended Kalamazoo Valley Community College in Kalamazoo, Michigan. I was concerned that I could not learn upon entry but became a 4.0 student in my first year. I was accepted into Phi Beta Kappa for excellence in my studies.

The University of Life:

- the study of Christ and the Christ consciousness
- the Buddha principles and how they work
- Center for Spiritual Living: the principles of Ernest Holmes on cause and effect, affirmative prayer, and *oneness*
- Unity Village: assorted classes on unity principles with deep-seated truths learned from Dr. Paul Hasselbeck, who teaches

the power of living within. Paul challenged me to change my thoughts by opening up, and thus changed my life once again.

- Lessons with Eckhart Tolle: the study of *The Power of Now* and *A New Earth*. Within this teaching I related to such a high degree that I found myself in service for the rest of my life. I nudge this information in my Phoenix Rising classes and retreats.
- Lessons with *The Four Agreements* and *The Fifth Agreement* by Don Miguel Luiz. I studied and practiced this teaching until I too could give it away to the listener that was ready. This is another nudging session taught in my Phoenix Rising classes and retreats.

Other sources of reference in the past four decades:
- the Bible and its teachings
- Deepak Chopra
- Eileen Cady
- Bill Wilson
- Ruth Montgomery
- Edgar Casey
- Wayne Dyer
- Eckhart Tolle
- Ernest Holmes
- the Fillmore's (founders of the unity principles)
- There have been many more teachers and classes that I have had the opportunity to explore. I listed the authors that have most inspired me.

Namaste! Please commune with the following.

It's All About You!
And This Time It's Okay

Have you ever been stuck? Have you ever wondered or worried about what the next right thing was for you to show up to? Not knowing what is next in our lives is something that plagues many of us. Learning to show up to the next right thing is something that I have had to learn through a process of many starts and stops. Finally after years of not being transparent and working hard to please the world, I started showing up to the next right thing, and I started trusting that the next right thing would reveal itself to me. As I did, I found the precious gift of living in the moment. After years of trying, I got a clear-cut message that if I wanted to keep all the lessons that I had learned, I would be required to give them away. I had listened, worked hard, changed the way I had been thinking, and was not going to relinquish the gifts I had received for being willing to show up to my life. It was this sacred awareness that caught my attention, and it was a moment of truth.

So without hesitation, with a great deal of willingness and faith, I started doing classes and retreats on staying in the present moment and showing up to the next right thing. Phoenix Rising was born. How apropos that this way of thinking was an exercise in change of thought and an opportunity for my own rebirthing once again. Phoenix Rising is the legend of a bird, living for three thousand years and traveling through the universe. When he comes to the end of his life, he cremates himself on a pile of sticks that were gathered with a sense of reverence and purpose. The phoenix then sets fire to the pile of sticks. The pile burns in a glory of tall flames, and the old bird disappears—but not for long. As the embers die, the young phoenix rebirths into his next lifetime as a young, strong, healthy bird with a soul ready once again for the adventures of the next three thousand years.

As a young boy, I read a children's book called *David and the Phoenix*. I was captivated from beginning to end. I too became the phoenix bird; I was constantly aware that I too had cremated my old ways of thinking and was rising once again from the ashes with a new thought. I was truly living in the moment, and it was time to give away the formula for this kind of blissful living. I became willing. I had faith in my journey. This information is for you. I want you to have what I have. It has been promised to all of us. I will share some of my journey, and I will share what I cremated and then what I rebirthed into my existence. This is not for a select few. We are one.

I became aware early on that I had nothing to teach but everything necessary in order to nudge people into their own awareness. I had learned that we all have the answers within. Telling anyone what to do with great authority may be effective temporarily, but it is soon forgotten. Without changing the way we think, our old ways of thinking come swiftly back. Nudging a group of eager people, who are ready to enlighten themselves with a new way of living, was my charge. I knew that if I put it out into the universe, the people seeking to know this truth would show up, and they did. Watching this new way of thinking change lives is the gift. I am committed to service for the rest of this lifetime, and I will be a 'nudger' for all who show up in my life. It worked for me, and I am sure that it will work for you!

So what *is* the next right thing in our lives that we need to put our attention to? What is it that we have been missing or too busy to catch in our daily lives? Many of us were missing so much that we were sleepwalking through our lives without seeing the beauty in everything we encountered. We just were not present. We thought we were, but upon further investigation it was obvious we were missing out on everyday living.

The process is not hard, but it has to be focused with awareness and intention and most of all, faith: faith that if we change the way we think, we will be changing the way we show up to everything. Everything will finally be the wholeness of all that we do and all that we are. To learn to show up to the next right thing can start with easy baby steps that get us ready for the big stuff. It can be as simple as calling a friend or having something to eat or as big as booking a vacation flight to London. It is whatever is in front of us that needs to be done in the present moment. By doing so, we get to do the next right thing, whether small or life-changing.

The classes and retreats that I have organized are based on nudging the participants into learning the art of listening, listening to their higher consciousness. At that juncture there is an answer that will come through: a transparent, truthful response, not as a solution to a problem, but rather by prompting a question that will give an answer. A certain feeling, usually in the heart chakra or in the pit of the stomach, will give us the answer to the question, "What is my next right thing to do?" So why not consider listening, with such a guaranteed outcome? Feel the answer in the silence, and lead with faith through any fear that arises, and the next right thing to be done is assured. It may be part of a few next right things to get to a final needed outcome. The universe does not recognize problems as a problem. Rather the universe is a positive thought. God is positive. The "I am" in us is positive with anything we say or do. This is why we have choices. A positive outcome is dependent on us, and we always get one by what we think, say, and do. Your God-self identifies opportunities and provides the answers to all of our questions. But this will only work if we learn to listen and communicate with our higher selves, our higher power, and the God of our understanding. Call it what you will, but just know that you have help from something much bigger than yourself.

By listening to our higher selves we are living in the land of our own opportunity, and if an immediate answer does not come, a feeling of peace and possibility can still fill our consciousness if we are willing to quiet down. The answer we are looking for needs to be in alignment with everything that is in front of us, and as a result we will not get the answer until we are part of a universe that works in perfect synchronicity. We can be assured that the answer will come to us in the simple step of showing up to the next right thing. Are you willing to take that first step of enlightenment? This is the first step in the journey of willingness.

My life has been filled with great authors and sages who showed up out of the blue right when I came into alignment and was ready to receive the information I was seeking and needing. I was miserable and desperately wanted to be happy and to learn to change my thinking. Ernest Holmes, who wrote the book *Science of Mind* as well as a series of other books, was invaluable to the next right thing in my life as a phoenix. He lectured for years and was a man of affirmative life principles. He changed lives, and lives changed because he taught how to affirm what was needed and thus expect an outcome because of cause and effect. God is the cause, and our choices through affirmation are the expectation of our positive choices. Mr. Holmes is among many other sages, authors, and spokespersons sending along the same or similar messages, from Jesus to Chopra, Edgar Cayce to Ruth Montgomery, the Fillmores of Unity Village to Mary Ann Williamson. The list goes on. We are blessed with many spiritual sages of the past and of the present to give us what we need. The message needed will always appear in front of us when we pose the question, have the awareness, and stand strong in the faith that we are here to know the answer to anything that will benefit us and the greater good. We are here to know the spiritual and scientific approaches to our lives, and to blend in our soulful spiritual self, which produces an automatic, cocreative, intuitive answer to our lives. It eventually comes forth to all seekers of truth that science and spirit are one. Everything we touch, feel, see, and know are one. There comes a time when we know that there is no separation.

Many of us may assume that this kind of thinking is something new. Many seekers are calling it *new thought*, but this formula of spiritual oneness has always been and will always be. We are at a point where many more souls are able to grasp this concept. Some are leaving organized religious dogma behind. There are others who need to be held accountable by a religious way of life. These souls are absolutely where they need to be for the time being. But if they start to question, they will receive universal direction as to the next right thing to do. If fear does not hold them back, they will be ready for the next dimension of higher thought. So if you are reading this book, you are ready to change the way you think! Be prepared to realize that you are not alone and that your intuitive, subconscious thoughts brought you here and are right on and shared by millions. Your Phoenix Rising rebirthing journey has begun. You are ready to tap into your intuitive nature and cocreate a life of peace, love, and service.

Within the past five years I have been captivated by the author Eckhart Tolle and his incredible read, *The Power of Now*. I became swept up with his now reality and how we can live in the present moment to claim our now life, which is the only way to find our peace. Amazing things can take place in our lives once the chaos of the monkey mind has settled down. The ego that is not our friend gets silenced for the first time when we live in the now. We start to feel our lives and to hear the small, still voice inside us. We are no longer bothered by an overactive ego.

In my experience of learning to live in the present moment I was excited to share this wonderful enlightened concept. For over twenty years I had read every teacher or sage that spoke of this concept. There was Depak Chopra, Eckhart Tolle, Ernest Holmes, as well as Ruth Montgomery, Wayne Dyer, and the list goes on and on, with way too many authors to mention. However, what I would like to say is that when I looked for the answer and asked, I received the answers. Once we pose a question to the universe we are inundated with all that we need to learn and all that we need to know. What a relief to get what we need! And as I learned, I found ways to nudge and share and work with others. I could give it away and touch other lives so that they too would feel the exuberance and freedom that I had discovered.

This information is no secret, and everyone has the same opportunity to access a personal relationship with an entity bigger than themselves. The words to define this entity are just words. Words, depending how they are used or interpreted, can do a great deal of good or a great deal of damage. When some hear the word *God*, they are disillusioned because of the judgments of religions that have followed that word. Words like *God* can sometimes make a person feel judged, scared, or unworthy because of what happened throughout history in the name of God and religion. So this is why we are not going to use just one word to define our relationship with our higher self. I personally do not have an issue with the word *God*, but that was not always the case. I can take that word and use it with many other words that I find to mean the same thing. So by getting past a word, we can access our needs with a power greater than ourselves. We can listen to the messages that contain the good and best interest for ourselves in any given situation and find the eye-opening, life-changing direction to doing the next right thing.

I have never assumed that this is an easy new way of life. Most of us have never even tried to change our thinking, let alone our years of past conditioning. We seem to have needed to take the long walk into the woods to find out what does not work, so that we could find what does. We are faced with egos that multitasked our brains with misinformation. It takes a great deal of courage and bravery to shut down this monster, the ego. We soon realize that the ego is not our buddy. We need to finally know that, so we can stop listening to voices that are not here to give us our lives, let alone a peaceful day.

Changing the way we think and live takes discipline, commitment and most of all the willingness to keep going. The great Winston Churchill once bellowed out his famous quote: "Never, never, never give up!" He was so right. Giving up is just not an option if we want a gifted, well-intended and successful life.

In the beginning of this awesome change, we are faced with a gaggle of lunatics in our heads that are nothing but freeloaders and disrupters. They feel very real because we have made them real. They want full control, and for most of us they succeed without us even being aware that they are sucking us dry and stealing our good energy. We may be attempting to make a good, positive decision, but we are suddenly faced with the illusion of doubt and fear instead of the feeling of ease that creates our ultimate success.

This is true sabotage. The ego wants full control. Some will argue that there is a healthy and an unhealthy ego. I am not going to dispute that theory. For most of us the healthy ego rarely gets the edge over the unhealthy ego. With healthy self esteem the ego seems good and is not too controlling. However, the ego that loves to show up seems to be one that is chaotic and fearful. This is definitely not an ego of health and wellbeing.

There are true signs that show us if we are dealing with a healthy ego or one that is running rampant in our thoughts. Our lives seem—and most often are—out of control, and our energy is depleted. We have a total lack of peace when we have an ego that is running amuck. The unhealthy ego is not our friend and is not going to let us off the hook. We soon understand that the unhealthy ego is the biggest chatterbox, turned up to full volume, and sometimes even speaking in tongues.

If ever in your life there was a self-appointed judge, you will find it in the unhealthy ego. It wants full control and has a lot to say about everything that has absolutely nothing to do with the present moment. The good news is that it is in the present moment that we catch this culprit and have opportunity to shut the ego down. It does take a decision to suit up in our spiritual warrior battle gear. This is where we make the choice to take out the energy-sapping ego.

If you have ever become aware of your personal judgments—and we all seem to go there—you will see that after a closer look, the judgments that we make about ourselves are acts of sabotage and self-induced fear. These are not of God or by God or for God. These are our own misrepresented thoughts, of the ego. The ego is never in our best interest. We can put ourselves on death row in an instant, or we can talk back to the negative ego with an affirmative statement. For example, "Oh, it's you again! You are not welcome here anymore and I must release you."

But in this moment we can be paralyzed with fear, and the mind just does not want to shut down. The what-ifs and the shoulds show up and are one more sign that the unhealthy ego wants to play higher power again. This becomes a turning point, and it becomes in our best interest to affirm who our higher power really is. Who has the power here? We have the power to claim what we know is truth. Any good, affirmative mantra works, such as, "All is well," "Trust the unfolding," "Just show up," and "Keep walking forward." Mr. Ego is totally disempowered.

Now that we know what to look for, we can have some fun naming our ego anything that we want to identify this with, for our own instant recognition. I have coined the Dysfunctional Board of Directors. My board does not want to shut up. They think they are always right, are diffident, and want me to constantly defend them. Because they are always right, and want to be defended, my conversations with them prove to be a total waste of time. No one listens to me, and if they do they are combative proving their own points. I walk away a winner only to realize I am a loser in the end. I cannot shut them down unless I am willing to go after them one by one. They chatter. They point fingers. They have resentments and get angry.

They are also avid moviegoers. They love to make their own movies about our lives and how they will play out. Their endings are typically full of drama and quite disastrous. After just a few minutes, if we are listening and watching, we can become so fearful that it's hard to move, let alone think. We are so far out of the present moment that there is only one thing left to do, so wanting my peace that there is finally only one thing left to do: "You're … you're out of here!"

At this moment Nirvana sets in and good power and control have returned. We find ourselves breathing and recognizing that we have returned to sanity and the present moment.

We discover that we are in charge of our own script and our own movie. We are the stars and we are willing to play the present moment's scene to the best of our ability. We live with change, updates, and great expectation, and we do so in the present moment.

We refuse to play the victim or live in a world of self-loathing, misery, and chaos. We are the cure of this *dis-ease*. All of us have the ability at any time to tap into the oneness. If we are willing to consider, open up, and become willing, great new territories will unfold that we had somehow missed on our journey.

So instead of turning to addictive behaviors to settle down the ego, there is an opportunity that will work in the now and for a lifetime. We get this wake-up call because we are worth it. We only have to listen. Sound easy? It is not too easy in the beginning to listen to the still, small voice that lives within us and has the answer, and is willing to make a commitment. But once commitment sets in, our lives will never be, and can never be, the same.

For many of us there are some years that just don't work. These can be considered good years. They bring us to a point of surrender. We would never surrender without the pain of a life that does not work. It takes what it takes and the blessings and gifts that come out of it are truly amazing and we come to realize that this is our birthright. So if misery is your game, oh well! It will either get better or worse and with either comes that opportunity to change. Taking a chance at peace seems like a no-brainer when actually it has nothing to do with brains but rather with our willingness to change the way we think. This new way of thinking is the bud of the rose that is finally ready to start blooming. We finally get our own spring season—the real one.

With spring comes a welcome change. If fear sets in, take a look at it. Observe it but do not participate in it. Fear works closely with the ego and wants to rear its ugly head when there is a positive change of consciousness. Fear, it is interesting enough to know, can be a motivator. It may even help us jump to the next right thing more quickly. But this is no longer fear. The still, small voice does the rest. We become ready to jump into our new way of thinking and our new life.

With many of us losing faith because of fear, it is interesting that at the edge of the abyss we are showing up to God, our higher power, and our higher consciousness. At a moment's notice we want to be sure that something bigger than us is going to save the day. But what we fail to realize is that in the oneness of the universe we always were connected. We were never anything but a part of God, even when we let the ego tell us we were better on our own. We are finally ready to have that private, confidential conversation with the God of oneness. We can thank this power that lives within all of us for not judging us the way we judged ourselves.

We can thank God for bringing us to our knees and letting us find out what no longer works in our lives, so that we can find out what does. Then we can look around, and for the first time know that no one, including ourselves, is ever left out. We are now ready to show up and jump with exhilaration into the next right thing. And our lives are continually full of the next right thing.

If you are still a doubting Thomas, that's okay! You still get the chance and opportunity to change that thinking. Hopefully you do not need to hurt anymore. Hopefully you want the relationship with your higher self so that you can be assured you are on track and that you can live with purpose. So, keep showing up. Keep paying attention. Keep your eyes, ears, and hearts open for the next right thing. Unless you really try to miss it, you just won't.

Mandatory Evacuation of the What-Ifs and the Shoulds

For many of us there has been a lifelong neighbor in our neighborhoods. The shoulds and the what-ifs can almost be like family. That could be a lesson in itself. They are testy and persistent and downright irritating.

There comes a time to pack them up and get them on their way. This mandatory evacuation becomes necessary for our ultimate well-being. In my own personal journey I finally noticed that they were not the friendly type and had been staring me in the face for most of my life.

There had been times when they actually stopped me cold from moving on. I wondered, in my moment of realization, about all that I had missed because of the what-ifs and the shoulds—those bastards! I had come to realize that it was time to come to showing up to the next right thing and get rid of these testy irritating neighbors. They had to go!

So as they were going, a relative showed up. Fear gripped me: "What if the what-if's and the shoulds came back, and would they ever really go away?" How real were these neighbors living in my head? And why did they seem to live everywhere I went and in everybody else's head as well? Were they talking in everyone's head, giving advice and comments? Then again, did I ever really listen to anyone else's advice for me anyway? I always did what I wanted to do, right or wrong, and usually out of an ego-filled command. Yet again I found myself at another crossroads on my journey. The what-ifs and the shoulds could no longer be ignored. A new way of thinking and a decision as to their destiny in my life had to be made. So I put them on notice. I wanted these pesky neighbors evacuated, and I seemed to be ready to let them go.

But were they ready to go? Or rather, were they so grandfathered into my consciousness that it was going to take an act of God to get them going? Yes, it was just that: an act of God! I began to try everything to delete them from my thoughts.

The moment had arrived and I was finally willing to do whatever it took. What was the magic potion that would gas them out? I got quiet, asked the question, and the answer came in a still, small voice connected to my higher self, the God of my understanding. I was the guy that had the power. With the help of the oneness of the universe I believed that the shoulds and the what-ifs could be removed. Imagine that! I no longer needed to be caught under their spell.

I committed to change and knew I would have to stay in the moment if I was to hear how to let these testy neighbors go. I also found out that as long as I stayed in the moment they could not gain entry. They left immediately when I took away their power. And when they kept coming back just to see if they could get in again, I reminded them that my door was closed and that the relocation out of my life had already taken place. Their homestead had been redeveloped.

As for my dear family and friends who had always been there for me with the what-ifs and the shoulds, I let them all know that the what-ifs and the shoulds were excommunicated from my life! Many friends and family had not yet let the shoulds and the what-ifs move to another neighborhood. They just were not ready. I knew that it had taken me years to even recognize they were there and that it would take whatever it took for my loved ones to be willing to get them out of their lives too.

We intuitively learn that we have to stand guard, and we do this by showing up to the next right thing. We finally realize that we are no longer asking someone else to give us the answers. Our discussions change and become about what is going on in our lives and about the opportunities we have had presented to us. At this point we find we are staying open to all suggestions. We come to realize that the universe absolutely talks through others. God shows up and talks through people. We need to listen. There is an old Buddhist principle that states if we stand still the doing gets done. When in the presence of our own lives we can often find that our listening skills come in just standing still— allowing the message that needs to be delivered to come through.

There had been a time in my life where I stuffed my emotions and used alcohol to medicate. It worked. I got so medicated that I had no sense of my own reality. What started out to be a temporary reprieve from life became an obsession of my mind. For years I had felt that I would never live past the age of forty. I was going to die. My affirmation came true but differently than I had stated. I had a total death of what I had previously known. My old life was gone, and I was rebirthing to a new journey. Like the phoenix bird, I was starting over. I had to change one thing, and that one thing turned out to be everything. As I began to show up to my life without alcohol, the what-ifs and the shoulds worked overtime, trying their best to work with my ego to sabotage my new life. They were relentless, but I had help. I had a spiritual connection that was a far greater power than they were. When in fear, I came to realize that if I listened to the wrong message I would lose the opportunity and the gift of having the life I was born to have.

In the process, I was engrossed in a deeply spiritual set of twelve steps used in the Alcoholics Anonymous program. That program started with my life at the beginning and brought me to the new life I have today. I came into that program with a deep spiritual sense that makes it much easier. For those who have to find God and their spiritual connection, the process of living is much more difficult, and staying sober is almost unobtainable. AA was a great help with the rebirthing process. It gave gifts immediately. I surrendered my old self and my real self emerged from the ashes of an old life that had shown me what would not work in the greater scheme of things.

But with impeccable truth I have known that I needed every drink I drank. After years of living in an abusive home, being depressed, shy and totally unsure of myself, alcohol gave me the life I never had. I became social, fun, and connected to a crowd of drinkers and party people. I needed it, and I still am grateful that something broke the ice for me. That was thirty years ago, and today I am substance-free. The difference is I can do everything I did drinking and more. I no longer need a mood-altering substance to be the life of the party. I surrendered my disease to God a long time ago, and I have no desire for a drink. It does not even cross my mind. I have friends that drink sensibly and I have my beverage of choice. I can go in a bar, down an aisle in the grocery store and I hardly pay any attention to what is on the shelves or behind the back bar. When I asked for this obsession to be taken, it was.

I no longer call myself an alcoholic because I am no longer a man that drinks to excess, or drinks at all. Calling myself an alcoholic seems negative and not truthful. What I do know is that if I were to drink again, with my family background and my family history, I would become an alcoholic. The rooms of AA would not agree with me on this thought process. But for me and my higher connection with the oneness of the God of my understanding, I know that for me, because of my surrender and the trust and the faith that I have learned, alcohol worked for a while and now is not needed. When you have a personal relationship with the God of your understanding it would take great effort to turn around and relive a past that had nothing to do with the present moment. Food, drugs, sex, gambling and anything else that is addictive sooner or later turns into the opportunity for change.

We all arrive with a pure and healthy soul. We have a fresh start no matter how many lifetimes we have incarnated. But with us we bring the past that has been unhealed and we are blessed to have yet another opportunity getting closer to what I call *the Christ consciousness* in my belief system. I want to have the opportunity to continue on a path that teaches me the perfection and the nirvana of the Christ and the Buddha. I came to realize early on that my soul came disturbed and needing some lessons in truth. I became willing as soon as I was willing. With soulful attention, the heart is nudged into the truth. We have to do what we have to do so that when the nudging comes, we have a chance to make a choice and to be willing. Finally our answers come, and we experience incredible strength to move through what we thought would be difficult and foreign to us. It would be shown to me by living intuitively that the answers I had been seeking had always been with me and were living from within. Faith became my key to my new kingdom. This was an old kingdom but new for me.

Essentially choosing a new way of thinking is, as Ernest Holmes so eloquently teaches, to have a changed thought system. Baby steps will always help at the birth of this journey. Starting a journey of learning to let go of self-judgment is done by learning to stay in the present moment. It all starts with intention. And there are no scorecards or comparisons needed. Starting over is always an option because to start over is a sign of good intentions, commitment and strength.

I left work one day after I had a day that was stressful, convoluted, and crazy. I was at my wits' end. I got in my car, went home, took a shower, made some coffee, meditated, and went back to work, saying my affirmations. I got back to work, sat in my desk chair and broke out into an insane laugh. What a great day that was.

My best days are the days I am aware in the moment of where I am and what I am thinking. Showing up changes us so we can start to live our life differently. I remember that I got the suggestion that I take a different way to work and change my daily routines and habits. I saw sights like trees, water and buildings that I had never seen before. It was a delightful experience and when in later weeks I took my original route, that I had taken for years, I saw so much that I had never seen before. I was beginning to live in the present moment. And as my life began to change, I was saying good-bye to some of my old friends and hello to some new friends. I was attracting like minds. It was all good!

Spiritual seekers of all walks of life have taught that when thoughts change, we change. When fear is gone, freedom shows up. The ego is only empowered with our help and with a changed thought system we get the opportunity to break cycles in our lives that no longer work. By doing so, and without even a word, we are role models for those around us.

Ernest Holmes teaches cause and effect along with many other modern day sages. Cause is God, and effect is what we affirm to our higher consciousness. To me this means I am part of the cause, as God lives within me. I tap in and change my present daily life by affirming what I already know I can have. This was a life-changer and I was no longer begging God for my good. My good was already available just with my recognition of where my good came from. I love being one with God and the results are far too many to list. I believe spirit cocreates with us when we are in the moment and have the willingness and the faith to show up to the gifts that await all of us for the taking. We may have anything that is beneficial to ourselves and others. We alone determine if each day is going to be spirit-guided. It's a real show-up moment.

Shovel Out The Caca: Clean Your Stables!

Transparency is a learned trait and a great way to find out who we really are and where we have been. I hesitated to share some of my journey, but the hesitation did not last long because of my commitment to being transparent. We all have stables to clean and I surely am not to be left out. I have been cleaning my stables for a long time. The only difference today is that I clean the caca out everyday instead of waiting for years. Can you imagine? So here is just one of my days at the stables, long ago when I was in my late twenties.

To set this story up, I would like to admit that my ego-filled life before enlightenment wanted to tell the whole truth, nothing but the truth, so help me God. But I did not. I came to realize that I was the teller of half truths. I justified this fear-based behavior as a way of not letting anyone really know me. I was afraid that if someone knew who I really was, I would not be liked or loved or accepted. I wanted brutal honesty from everyone else but I was not willing to be totally truthful myself. I just did not know how and I was not willing to change that way of thinking. And yet I had my best friend's parents loving me unconditionally. Bob and Mick Bayer gave me such a sense of worth, and I never could understand why. They saw so much more in me than I did. As I grew older, they were right and were still loving me as a son. But as we all need to do at some point if we want to have a life, I eventually I had to change, so I could have a chance at being authentic.

I no longer wanted to be untruthful—I wanted to always tell the truth. But when one has been hiding for decades, the truth is what comes out of your mouth because this is what you begin to believe about yourself and others.

I was not only untruthful; I also embellished stories for comic effect. What a hard lesson to learn! Today I am a comic with a repertoire of truth. It works much more easily. My most confidential information now goes to a select few, like-minded people. Fortunately with their own strong spiritual commitment, they listen without taking anything personally. I am not judged. I do not judge. We have a relationship of trust and a solid friendship. We do not repeat anything discussed. Well, not that I know of. We do nothing to intentionally hurt another soul. Our intentions are in the best interest of each other with this shared information. Our intent is not to hurt anyone, including ourselves. But all of us need a confidant to share our thoughts, dreams and temporary disappointments.

As my valuable lessons were presented to me, so were the people that were going to help me get through them. I received a great deal of guidance from ancient teachings, new thought authors, and the still, small voice that I had finally learned to access. That voice had always been with me but I had never sought the answer to unlock this treasure chest. I started showing up to my life. I found spiritual centers, unity churches, support groups, and anything that was going to be good for me to know or learn. I went back to school, and finally got some college behind my belt.

I was realizing that in crisis, I was always at the door of opportunity. Of course I had to learn this on my own. God forbid anyone try to tell me that until I was ready. The right people were always in front of me. I needed to recognize that they were there. I started taking a chance by finding out. What I thought was an accident, was a right on time moment for me to have exactly what I needed. Some call this a miracle, and for awhile I did too, until I realized that the miracle was that I recognized what was in front of me. I became my own miracle.

Along the way, I came across another author that shared and taught me so much in a small, simple book called *The Four Agreements*. His name is Don Miguel Ruiz. At the time I read the book, I was caught in a hallway; one door was open yet and I had not closed the situation. I was fearful and waiting as if someone else was going to close that door. No one showed up. The other door was open for me to enter. It enticed me with new living, curious adventures, new people to share my life with and new opportunities. I knew that I had to close the door behind me before I could get out of that long, lonely hallway. I had to become willing and I needed help. I asked for help and it came to me in *The Four Agreements*.

These are the four agreements that challenged me to make a positive change in life:

1. Be impeccable with your word.
2. Do not assume anything.
3. Do not take anything personally.
4. Always do your best.

The Four Agreements really hit home. My ego loved it. I had always done my best, or so I was being persuaded to believe by my ego. No, I was not doing my best. I had to have a contract with myself and my higher power to commit to the other three agreements and then I had a chance at doing my best.

My early adult life had not been run by these agreements. I admit that at the time I realized this, I felt some shame, remorse, and had a little pity party all by myself. Up to this point I had not realized how dishonest I had been.

All and all, I gained some insight about the courage it takes to make changes. I was ready to embrace yet another set of changes. By telling others what they wanted to hear and not telling them everything about me, I left out some important truthful dialogue that would build a lasting committed friendship or love relationship.

I had fooled myself and I had thought I had fooled others. But had I? I had years of hiding from myself. My hiding was done so perfectly that when I needed myself for important decisions, I was nowhere to be found.

Where does one pick up this thinking? It was time to look back and take time to do an inventory. I needed to start at the beginning. Being ashamed of my family life and the drama that unfolded because of it, I found myself not sharing anything about my young life. I kept much of it buried in my sub-consciousness and was not willing to discuss it or even confront what it had emotionally done to me. We do not have to live the life of our childhood until we die, but we need to accept what has happened, forgive it, and move on. In fact, it is *so important* to acknowledge what happened, why, and just move on. The past is the past and in the end, unless we let it affect our present moment, it can no longer be a disabling factor in our present moment happiness.

I came from an abusive childhood. The whole experience growing up was abusive. This was true. This was my secret. But anyone that knew my family already was well aware that 1643 Shangri La Drive was a house of horrors. Once out of the house at age sixteen, I had escaped and was not talking. I finished high school, had two jobs and was once again rescued by my girlfriend's parents. I moved in with them and had a chance to see a family having fun. They had their problems too but it was a paradise in comparison to what I had lived through. I still kept close tabs on my mother but I was detaching. As much as I wanted to be her knight in shining armor and protect her, without knowing it I was detaching. Her loyalties were not with me when there was a choice for her to have peace with my father. I never faulted her for that. Later in my life I realized how deeply connected we were over many lifetimes. I loved her with all my heart and still do and always will. I finally realized that as a child of abuse and secrets, I had been taught to hide and not give out truthful information. A family that lives in secret produces a life that turns into more secrets. I wanted to break that pattern. But how?

My secrets continued into my early twenties with a marriage to a young lady that came from a healthy family. But I was living a secret. I was a gay man who needed an alternative lifestyle. I kept my secret well hidden from not only others but myself. Being gay in my early life was just one more black mark on the report card of life, in a world that was not accepting to an alternative life style. We married and we divorced in fewer than two years. I came clean with her because I fell in love with her after we were married. I wanted this precious soul to have what she needed too. I continued to stay underground with my secret for many years. I lived a double life. I was not true to myself or anyone else. I had no tools in my toolbox to figure out how to be authentic so I medicated with alcohol. It worked for a while but the day came where I was forced to come clean on everything.

In my thirties I tested the water with the truth about my sexuality. I was told that it was just a phase. My doctor suggested foreplay. My mother was sure it would pass. Even well into my forties I had friends that ignored that part of me and could not discuss it. I was the elephant in the room. I was invisible as to who I was. Even after I put down the wine and came clean on my sexuality, the elephant remained in the room with a few of my close friends.

I stayed in this state of numbness for many years and then at forty the game was over. I was dead. I was dead in the water. I was medicating with a drug that no longer worked. I checked into rehab against the will of others who were in denial as to my excessive use of alcohol. I began a new journey that was extremely bumpy at first but I needed help. In the process alcohol had saved my life by threatening to take it. It brought me to the gifts of transparency and authenticity. Priceless.

So my prophecy came true: at forty I died. It was a painful death. But I was rebirthing with a great deal of help. This help lived in the vapors I breathed. I was stone sober and things did not look good. I had not seen the world sober sense I was twenty-one. And even as a child I had lived in depression, rejection, and abandonment so I was totally unaware what the world was like and how I would have to learn to survive. I just was not prepared.

One of the biggest steps I had to take was to forgive myself. When I finally asked for help without guilt, I was carried and helped gently under a universal law, the law of love. I was coming clean. It hurt. It hurt like hell. But something deep inside me told me that it would be worth it. *Just show up* became my saving grace. I came to believe in something greater than myself. I was told that I would have a great life if I surrendered to a power greater than myself. I had been hiding from God as well, and yet in my heart of hearts I knew that I wanted to go home and get the guidance and the help from a forgiving and loving God. I needed to find that God because the one I grew up with hated me—or so I thought.

Looking back, I do have a story to share about my "old self" that I can tell today without too much painful embarrassment. It was a time for me when I wanted to be everyone but myself. I was twenty-nine years of age and going on a cruise to the Bahamas with my dear friend Margaret. She and I worked together, and I had known her for quite some time. Margaret was in her late fifties and wanted to join me on a month-long vacation that we got every year. She knew I was fun and living edgy. She was doing some rebirthing herself. She cut her hair, lost fifty pounds and planned a vacation with me. I loved this gal and she loved me and the gossip from all the chatty women we worked with just fueled the fire that we had started. Margaret was going to spend her vacation with me, thirty years her junior. As for my sexuality, it never came up. I did not tell her and she assumed that I was a straight guy. I let her have that assumption happily. Margaret was German-born and had a lovely accent that many found endearing, including myself. She was charming to be with, and we had become good friends over the years that we had worked together.

But it was my vacation too, and I was still playing in my sexual underworld. I was hiding who I was but always looking for someone that I could have a quick fling with. I met a young guy my age from Australia and found him to be charming, handsome and maybe like me, but I was not sure. Was he gay? Or was he not? How was I going to find out? I wanted him to really like me, as I was very attracted to him and his great accent. So I became a Danish immigrant living in the US and on vacation. I took on a broken Danish accent. He was taken aback and became quite attentive. I spent a great deal of time with him on the cruise. I also needed to spend time with Margaret and did not want her to think I was spending time with anyone else. So I maneuvered the situation—speaking broken Danish to my Australian friend, and having meals with Margaret where I spoke English and she spoke her broken English. Then back to my Australian connection I went, speaking brokenEnglish with a Danish accent again. Needless to say, I was exhausted and sometimes quite confused. I caught myself saying something to Margaret in broken, Danish-accented English. Oh boy!

Today I would so like to come clean with my Australian connection that shared time with me on the cruise. It was a long time ago and I have looked for his address but to no avail. I even looked for one of the letters he sent me thirty years ago. I am just hoping and praying that when I finally do get to make my amends, he tells me that he was really an Italian faking an Australian accent!

Today I live by the four agreements that I referenced earlier. I am not hiding, pretending, or playing a game with anyone. I am just being who I am in the present moment and if I slip a little, I catch the slip, apologize and start over. First, impeccable—today I have many people that love me and count on me to *be impeccable*. I honor that commitment and there is no turning back now.

When it comes to *assumption*, I know I cannot read your mind. I have no assumptions anymore. I need to know the facts, and I am willing to wait for all that needs to be said or done. At that juncture I can make my own healthy conclusions. By being an excellent listener there is nothing to assume. By learning about what I am told, I am equipped to show up to the next right thing. This may well be a statement of intent or truth. But it is not an assumption without dialogue. With the gift of being *impeccable*, and not *assuming*, it becomes almost impossible to take anything personally.

Not taking things *personally* is a huge accomplishment. I have desensitized and let go of my fragile ego that would love me to feel like a piece of caca without good reason. If there is something that hits me wrong, I will let you own it. Most times a person that is sending out barbs or misinformation is doing it to themselves. It becomes an attempt to self-correct. There is an easier softer way. Breathing deeply will always slow a process of quick responses as this is a true moment of being in the present. This is a learned technique in meditation and it works to access that still, small voice that always has the answer.

By being willing to clean our own stables, we are given our *best* days. A 4.0 day is *doing your best*. And I know many people that need to be 4.0 people including myself. But it is more than a scholastic grading system. It is about doing our best. My best is always good enough even on my 2.8 days, when I have gone as far as I can go and have to be accepting of the fact that I have done my best for the day. Without a second thought I know in my heart that I have done my best and had a 4.0 day. This new self-taught dynamic to living in the now has left self-judgment without the power to steal my peace.

So *do your best* all the time and remember that your best changes from moment to moment. Even so, it can still always be your best.

Our Past Is Today's Opportunities "So click your heels and get on with it!"

The classic film called *The Wizard of Oz* was not supposed to be the success that it has become. But by looking a little closer at the storyline, it is understandable that such a subliminal spiritual message has captivated audiences for decades.

Dorothy is whisked away in the turbulence of a tornado from her life as it seemed to be—a question of not knowing how much she was loved. She is taken to a land far from home and now is on the quest of returning to her loved ones. Once not home, all she could think about was how to get home. Sound familiar? She did have little dog, Toto, with her to remind her of how much love she had to give. Toto was a representation of the unconditional love we have for others. The message is clear that the way home is by a deep surrender and listening to our hearts. Dorothy was on the weave of the yellow brick road, symbolizing a journey of learning and adventure. Like Dorothy, we too face the road before us where we are in search of the right road to Oz, where the answers we are seeking will present themselves. So what does it take, and does anyone get out of the journey? I think not. As it was told in *The Wizard of Oz*, the adventure included trials and tribulations, bad witches and good witches, and the illusion that great Oz had the answer. But who was the great Oz? Was he really going to save Dorothy and will he save us if we ever find him? Was Dorothy saved by the great Oz or was she saved by the surrender and the trust and the faith that brought her safely home? Flying monkeys, befriending munchkins, and the search for the ruby reds were the ways she traveled in time to find her way back home. She came to realize that she had the answers within and that home was where the heart is. So what does it take to catch our attention so we too can go to the heart and find our life's purpose in the moment?

Letting go of what cannot be changed can sound simple. But once we get the message of surrender, we find that our old ways seem to be an easier way to travel through time. Or is it easier in the end to change our old ways? Old ways that no longer worked or have never worked need to be changed. It will prove to be the easier softer way. Opportunity proves that changing our old ways, changing our thought system to embrace mind, body, and spirit, is a road to our heaven on earth.

Our past is the past for a reason. We are never going to have the same past twice. It may be similar but it will never be exactly as it was. It is gone. Our past becomes the opportunity of a lesson that will deliver us to the life we are supposed to be enjoying. Without learning what does not work, we are unable to have a choice of what will work. Our past is full of gifts along the way. Everything we decide, everything we do, is all part of the way we are showing up, and it is important that we do so with intention. When intention is involved, we live in the moment and our past becomes, for the most part, a friendly memory or a dreaded thought. But whatever it is, it is gone. By observing what does not work, we have already started on our own yellow brick road to Emerald City. We begin to fall in love with ourselves, our families and our friends. We begin to be more compassionate and we start to look at life much differently because our thinking is changing. We become willing to take the journey of recognizing oneness. Sometimes it takes a disaster, drugs, alcohol, food, financial loss, or the loss of a loved one to catch our attention. As long as we are awakened to the truth of who we are by changing the way we think, we are on a road that promises us the change we are seeking. We begin to lose resentments, self-judging, comparisons and anger. How odd this feels at first! But we need to know that the journey is not over until it is over, and there will be ups and downs and sometimes we may even feel as if we are sideways. But somewhere along the way we actually end up embracing change. We even look forward to it. We find that change is natural and consistent with the flow of life. We join that flow instead of resisting it. Fear in our past becomes our teacher instead of a motivator to continue the same old ways of getting the same old results. If we fight change, we are either ready to check out or ready to live a living hell. Change is what happens while you are alive. Being alive means living fully in the present moment and showing up to the excitement of the next right thing in front of us.

Showing up to opportunities is the gift. We find that if we are willing to embrace everything in the now, we are actually building a future of nirvana without even realizing it. The future we are building in the now is not stressful or lusted after. It just happens because we are finally open to the listening that will guide us to the next right thing.

There will be no finding fault in ourselves because we are done finding fault with everybody else. But it does take starting with ourselves. Our now-moments do not play with the past nor the future. We become focused and are no longer concerned with anything that we have no control over. We are into living. We want the now and we want all of it without distraction. And if we want to put good intention out for our future, we can do that because we are building it one day and one moment at a time. We now are living in the expectancy of the good. So with the work that needs to be done, we get the heart that the Tin Woodman was looking for. He too found out that always had a heart. He just needed to recognize it. The Cowardly Lion had been searching for courage and in the end he too found that it lived within. Now the Scarecrow was determined to have a brain. His brain was nothing to seek. He had a brain and he proved it well once he realized his potential, using not only his brain, but also his heart, and courage, and his love for Dorothy

The heroine of this great story is Dorothy, who leads the compassionate charge of helping others. The principle that giving and receiving are the same was very apparent as she weaved through the journey with her traveling companions. They proved to be not separate but one. Oneness is the big message in this classic tale. Dorothy had a quest. She needed the ruby reds to get home. She could only have the ruby reds after she overcame adversity, and she did so with a change of thinking. She started listening to her heart. She had to have faith. She knew that when she clicked the ruby reds, it was not the Wizard of Oz and his fear tactics that got her home. It was purity of heart. And when she arrived by waking up, she was greeted by all of her loved ones. She got the global homecoming. Everyone was there. Her dream was real. So on our way home with our dreams we find we will have traveled a long way. In the end, and hopefully well before our end, we do have the opportunity to return home. And home is where the heart is. We find that safe place when we are living in the moment. Addressing any issue, any change, or any request becomes so much easier. Otherwise we are far too busy looking back and then looking ahead to all that is gone or all that has never even happened yet. We find ourselves in the company of humanity at its best, here in a loving soulful journey. It will be obvious that we are attracting likeminded souls. We will have the same ecstatic wake up that Dorothy had and we will be sharing the good that we have learned to recognize. Our lessons become acknowledged, and we once again move on to the next right thing.

If our past continues to chatter away, we get to make the choice to settle down and let the unhealthy ego leave our day. It absolutely becomes our choice. That is the biggest lesson we learn: how to have choices.

There will come a time when you will not want to miss anything in your moments. And when learning to move on to the next right thing, it will become important to your emails and phone calls. And when asked to participate in someone's life by accepting an invitation, it is so powerful to say, "Yes I will. Yes I can." Saying yes to anything good fulfills previous intentions. It also becomes not only a courtesy but a necessity to shut down your phone. Paying attention to who is in front of us honors the person and the moment. Learn the art of listening, for it serves us well when making heartfelt decisions. I always try to remember that the Road Runner never gets there first. Slowing down has stopped the insanity of repeating tasks and old behaviors.

Our unhealthy ego loves to be in charge of our chatter. It makes us feel so important at times, like we have multiple answers for everything and everybody. But giving ourselves some quiet time and a deep breath gives us what we need, and other people's lives are none of our business. We are here to listen, learn, and love. That is our support system for those we love. It takes practice listening to the heart but it will accomplish the mission of shutting down the ego. It is worth it!

If we find ourselves looking to everyone else instead of ourselves for answers, this becomes an immediate wakeup call. It is a call that we need to practice looking for. If someone else is looking for faults and is judging us, it is important that we learn to spot these energy vampires. Just letting them go without a huge reaction is the tool in our toolbox that will keep us drama free.

Looking back at my early years, I remember the struggle I had not to pick up a drink, which was my drug of choice. What started out to be a means of medication in order to be social had finally turned on me and had become the beast. Surrender is the first step to recovery. I had to acknowledge that I had a problem with alcohol. When that sunk in, I began working the program of Alcoholics Anonymous and I did so diligently. As I got better, my ego kicked in and I was on a roll. I knew it all, and I had all the answers. But of course I was wrong and had to have a few wake up moments along the way. There were many lessons of life to learn sober, and I was just like everyone else that had hidden behind my addiction.

Here is a story about a relationship I had in the rooms of AA that gave me a gift in disguise. Remember my social skills were nil prior to drinking, and when I stopped drinking I was raw to life on life's terms. I had no coping skills and a lot to learn. Every experience including the one I am going to share helped.

All of us in the rooms of AA, when first arriving, were very fragile. Most of us still smoked heavily and drank gallons of coffee to calm our nerves. Ha! I met a gal that was coming off alcohol and prescription drugs. We struck up a friendship and did some socializing. We both were trying to learn a new way of living and the roller coaster ride was one we were both on. We helped each other by talking about the ride. We both attended many meetings and were committed to staying sober one day at a time. On one particular afternoon, after the noon meeting at the Alano Club, I overheard my friend say that she had a year in. Wow, that was news! That was big news and quite an accomplishment. I immediately walked over and congratulated her, not expecting what happened next. Rage was on her face and she was screaming at me that I had no right listening to her conversation or assuming that she had a year of sobriety. She had been talking about pills not alcohol. I was hit hard with this ambush and began feeling all the emotions that I used to feel under the ambush of a confrontation. I would always turn to my buddy alcohol, the finger pointing, or rage of another person. I always drank until I passed out so I did not have to feel anything. If I had not been committed to recovery at that time, I would have easily gotten drunk to kill the pain.

The rage did not stop there. I got a series of threatening phone calls that she was going to "out me" on my job, which was helping an older lady in the neighborhood with yard and household work. And my AA buddy did just that. I got the call that my services were no longer needed. She had heard that I was an alcoholic and that I would rob her blind. I became obsessed with the chatter in my head, and I wanted to take revenge. I was hurt and infuriated. Between my depression and my anger, I was ready to get this gal back. She had shared some very personal information with me about an affair she was having with a prominent married man in the community. I was still green and had not learned that when someone was pointing there are four pointing back at the one who is accusing. So I made the call to her that even drinking I most likely never would have done. I threatened her with retaliation and told her that I was going to place a call to her lover's wife and call him out at his place of business. He was a banker and well known in the community.

The phone call scared her and sent her into a tailspin. It had worked. But I was not feeling good about what I had done. It felt both right and wrong at the same time. It made me more miserable. I shared this experience at an AA meeting in an attempt to let it go. And after I shared this topic not using names I settled back to listen like I had been told to do by my sponsor. Many agreed with what I did and saw value in the retaliation. Some even wanted to join in and bathe in the vengeance.

I was getting the wrong recovery message and I knew it. I was still miserable. I knew that this was not what true sobriety was, and I needed peace. I was in a spiritual program about changing my thinking and I had not done so—yet. I never made that call to her lover's wife.

It took about three months to get over what happened, and that was just around Christmas time. I had been struggling with the monkey mind reminding me daily at what this gal did to me. I found myself wanting to forgive her. She was not talking to me so I was not sure how to go about forgiving her without her thinking I had become holier than thou. Of course that was my stinking thinking. But with some quiet time and some thoughtful prayer and meditation, I got a glimpse and a feeling as to what I was to do. The holidays were upon us and I was doing my Christmas cards and found myself addressing an envelope to her. In the card I simply and sincerely wished her a very happy and joyous and peaceful holiday. I signed the card, I let go, I let God, and I moved on. And then again I let go, let God and moved on. And then again. Finally I let go. It was the first of many times that I would be finding ways to forgive and move on. I not only forgave her but forgave myself for the way I had reacted. It was the start of a life that did not react to the reactions of others. I had realized that this lesson was good for me and was about the gift of forgiveness, not vengeance. It was the lesson in letting go and moving on. Twenty three years later I am a master at letting go and moving on. I never want to ever feel the unhealthy energy around holding on to anything that I can let go of. I was embracing and connecting to the oneness that lives in all of us, and I was willing to change. What a great benefit to me!

Twenty years later I was back in the town where this all happened, and I ran into one of the AA people that had sided with the gal as to the way she went after me. We passed each other outside of a store; we both stopped and said hello. He wanted to know if I was sober and I told him I was. Then came the big, button-pushing questions: "Have you called Sally (a fictitious name) your friend to say hello? Have you seen her?" I looked at this man and immediately felt compassion. He was still twenty years in the past and thinking about that situation. He had not let it go. It felt as if he was trying to open a wound that I had healed years ago. And I noticed that he was holding on to his own participation in the situation. At the time he had made me feel very uncomfortable but that was twenty years ago. I remember looking at him and wanting to see his soul. I smiled and said, "No. I have not seen her, but what a good lesson she has been for me and I was hoping that she was having a good life." I said this to him without a thought of vengeance, or acting out. But because I now knew more about healing and soulful conversations, I let him have that thought for as long as he wanted to keep it. I did not defend myself or offer any inappropriate information on an event that was in my past and totally healed. It did remind me that I sent him a Christmas card as well with a message of love and peace. I said goodbye and have not even thought about this encounter until now. I write about this part of the experience because today I am healthy, and he and Sally taught me so much in the process of letting go.

This was a story about a past that was long gone and fortunately forgotten except for the lesson of what works in a real life situation without a mood altering substance. So what is the message here? You got lessons? Good! An excellent quote from Eileen Cady: "Learn your lessons and move on quickly." Click your ruby reds and keep moving. I did, and by doing so I have been able to show up to the next right thing over and over again. My buttons were no longer exposed to be pushed. It does take practice but I did have the time. I was seeing positive healing results from the lessons I had to experience. I am still learning. But now I have tools to fix myself. What an ah-ha moment!

Intention Means You Keep the Ruby Reds

Intention for me has proven that whether I put out a good or a bad intention, it will come to pass in the end. If I am putting out a good intention and start the process of showing up to the next right thing in my life, I start to see results. I have learned that for the final results everything around my intention needs to be in play. Like the tides, the stars, and the planets, along with the people involved, there is a rhythm that takes the bull by the horns and keeps me and everything around me in sync. My good intention will come to fruition. Waiting to show up is not an option when clarity is achieved. Future thinking does not help. Past failures or successes do not play into the way my good intention plays out. If anything, they will hinder the process.

Being free of procrastination gives us a clear, clean answer with a successful outcome, just the way it is supposed to be. However, sometimes we are guided to wait, and if we push forward anyway, the intention we had hoped for will not come to be in the way we had hoped. We once again got in the way of the law of cause and effect. This is not to be judged by myself or God. But it could be a missed opportunity that will only show up once in this lifetime. Listening once again to that still, small voice within lets us know whether we are to move or to wait. Remember, in some cases waiting is an action step. When the time is right, the message will appear, and that is when it will be time to move on.

All intention is positive. The universe only hears positives. If I say I am going to be sick, I can count on it. If I claim my health and prosperity, I can count on it. Whatever I proclaim, it is heard as a positive. So with that in mind it is good to think before speaking. Listen to the truth that lives in your still, small voice and move into an affirmation with the power of the heart.

My mother was great on stating the need to be positive. She preached that mantra, but it lacked the component that made it work. That component is consistency, knowing that we know and that we commit to keep going with the magic of faith. Action is the formula that allows positive thinking to work. Again it needs to be remembered that there will be times when inaction is as positive as action. Allowing a result to show up in the right time can be a nonaction step. However, there will be a need to show up to the next right thing as we allow this manifestation to unfold. Intention as the main focus will always produce results. When we state our intention, it has to be stated only once, and for the quickest result we must let go. But in letting go we still have the fun or expectation that the results are already done.

Part of my action in showing up to my day is a daily routine starting in the morning. No matter what time I have to be somewhere, I am always awake three hours prior to showing up. As I awaken, I find my chattering ego busy with multiple tasks relating to my work, my play, and the people that are in my life. This is my time to shut down the voices in my head and start the quiet time that gives me the answers. Also, I have some daily spiritual readings from Ernest Holmes that I absorb. Then there comes my time for affirmations regarding my daily life. I send out good intentions to all that I am and all that will be. I include my writing, my friends, my classes, and my family. If I know of someone who is struggling, I affirm their health and wellbeing. And my prayers are big because I believe in living globally. I want the universe and the people in it to have all that they need. It is now time to start my day, and I already know that it will be all that it needs to be. I take this time to feel connected and available for all that is ahead of me.

If I have a question that needs answering, I affirm that the answer will come at the perfect time as long as I stay in the moment. It may come to me via a billboard, a song on the radio, a phone call, or by running into a friend who happens to be carrying the answer to my question. As many of the prophets of old and modern-day sages have shared, the universe operates in positively, perfect, and synchronistic order. All of the movement is perfect and positive and on time.

I put out my intention, let go, and know that at the right time, in the right place, all will be revealed. It may be different in the way it plays out than I thought, but time will prove that it was the best for the greater good of all.

Affirmative thought allows the law of cause and effect to work. But what about others who are in front of us who do not have our best interest at heart? We once again have the opportunity to note the intention they bring, release a judgment of nonreaction, and move on. With as many lessons as all of us are learning, it behooves us not to take on someone else's negative bad attitude. We are far more helpful to the people around us when we are able to stay clear. A great deal of love can be dispersed by staying clear and sending compassion to those that are in need. After all, we all have those moments when compassion from another makes a huge difference.

If you have gotten this far in *Just Show Up*, you are never going to be the same. Once we have the information as to what we need to do, there is no turning back. We can try, but we are haunted with messages that we need to hear and put into practice. I am giving away this message. It is not a new message. No matter who gives it away, whether sages of old or our neighbor on the street, each person giving away this message is nudging someone at just the right time. My hope is that this is the right time for you and this is a message you can hear.

As we embrace this old thought that is new to us, there is one bigger shift needed: faith. Yes, faith that is not a fearful doctrine that dictates judgment and fear. Our faith usually has to start with small acts until we can get used to the idea that we have been under protection all along. And with faith and intention there are many successes. Faith lifts roadblocks, dispels fear, and relives worry about what has been and what is yet to come.

There will be times we are stopped by dis-ease, disease, accidents, loss of jobs or relationships, and the list goes on. Being stopped is the gift of opportunity. Finally something has stopped us so that we can have a look at where we are and why. After we get over the fact that we are stopped, insightful information will start to flow. Many times there is panic and fear. It needs to be felt and observed before we can let it go. We are at the crossroads of a new thought and possibly a new life. Faith in the process is what it takes to carry us through during turbulent times. Why me? Why not? We all get opportunity to reenter this life, letting go of who we were, to become who we really are.

Take a look behind that scary curtain where the great Oz is pushing buttons and pulling levers and see what is really there. From the outside, all you see is a dramatic light show and you hear all those levers being pulled and buttons being pushed and the fear sets in. Is he going to save me? But the great Oz is trying to save himself, just like our egos. Go ahead and rip down the curtain of fear, and you will find that it is an illusion. It is at this time that most of us get the chance to start connecting with something much bigger than ourselves. The Wizard was not the one we needed. The ego is not the one that has the answers. Emerald City was not the real estate we were really looking for. We wanted and needed to go home. And we are on our way when the fear fades into the midst of the poppies.

So you think that you misplaced your ruby reds? Don't worry. They are to be found, and they are for boys and girls, men and women. They are genderless just like your sunglasses. So the time is now and the ruby reds need to be slipped on so that you can click your heels, feel the moment, challenge your faith and be on your way! Choose how you will go: up, up, and away in your hot air balloon, clicking your ruby reds, or screaming out in the back yard, "Beam me up Scotty!" You now have the right to be totally outrageous. Because you get it! Just know you are on your way! You have been nudged! Just show up!

The Good And The Bad: Which Witch is Which?

Growing up with fables and tales of the good and the bad witch, we get the picture pretty quickly that, as in *The Wizard of Oz*, Glenda wants to give you what you want. She is a little fruity and sappy, but in the end she wants you to be happy. Just ask the good witch and your every dream and request will come true. But there is some work involved. Which witch is in your life? It would be good to realize that without the bad witches, we would not have a clue who the good witches are. We need things to not work in our lives so that we may accept the things that do work. Sometimes the good witch is evident in our thinking and sometimes the bad witch controls our thoughts. The bad witch has characteristics that are easily identified. She is the witch that challenges your every decision and says you can't when you know you can. She spreads fear and tales of lack. She tends to dislike anything that takes her out of her comfort zone. Right or wrong, she tells you not to move. She threatens your peace and she does not let up when pestering you to surrender. And the only good thing the bad witch does is to nag at you to surrender. But do we want to surrender to her ugly ideas and end up in her witch cave? She has not found out yet that true surrender is the answer to change and a new thought. It is her bucket of water and she will get it in the end. The bad witch also does not realize that she is powerless over true surrender. Her fate could be that one day she could turn into a good witch but it will take a lot of water to melt her down.

Once we are open to new ideas, new thoughts and in-the-moment living, we get the answers we need post haste. The bad witch has a twin that has been a longtime friend. They are inseparable. Born seconds apart the ego and the bad witch are joined at the hip.

The good witch, on the other hand, encourages and promotes positivity. There is nothing that can go wrong when you listen to the good witch, because even those things that look negative or wrong live in opportunity become the good we are seeking.

The good witch knows you have the resources within you to overcome any obstacle. She reminds you that there is nothing to fear. She speaks confidently and empowers you to find the answers within. She is one with your higher consciousness and is always on your side. The good witch will never lead you astray but will be part of your guidance system whenever you allow her to be.

Taking a breath and looking at past experiences in my own life, I can easily see that both the good and the bad witch have played major roles in catching my attention as to the way I choose how I will transform my life to be what I want it to be.

If fear is removed, I move into clarity of thought and enjoy prosperity in all that I do. I am willing to claim that I have all that I need. I live in expectation that there is more to come on the horizons. With this kind of thinking, I have proven in my own life, that under any circumstances I always have enough, if not more than enough. Let's just say I have not been hung out to dry.

When I am in need, Glenda the Good Witch shows up through a good friend or a gift from out of the blue.

I was living in Seattle when the country took a big economic hit in around 2006. I was working as an interior designer and offered my clients spiritual energy treatments for their homes. I was showing up daily and building a business that was struggling due to a struggling economy. I shopped at Safeway for my grocery needs. I was noticing that I was living very carefully and felt that the money seemed tight. I needed to claim my abundance and get rid of that negative thought. I proclaimed on a daily basis that I had all that I needed and more would be revealed. The work I was doing was slowing down and I got a clear-cut message one morning that I needed to go home to Michigan. I had always wanted to live in Seattle and I was sure that I was home. I asked why? Nothing came to me. But with my previous spiritual gifts of knowing that I know what I need to know, I listened and began to prepare to finish a project and move back to Michigan, on the shores of Lake Michigan. I sold some furniture, requested a container to fill and ship. I loaded up my most prize procession, my Airedale Terrier Goldie, in my car. A friend had come to Seattle to drive back with me. She was from Michigan and was my Glenda. I needed the help and the help was there.

The project I was working on ended. I had not been fully paid by two clients and had been misled to believe that I would get the money for services rendered. I did not receive what was mine and just let it go. I was trusting in an outcome that I was not in charge of. I received a call from Safeway that I had won first prize in a contest they were having. Would I please come to the store to claim my prize? I never win anything and thought that it was nothing much. I stopped by the store to pick up a gift in the form of a credit card that gave me $2,500 in gas that was good at any station in the country. Thank you, Glenda. Thank you for the out of the blue gift that helped me return home and once home gave me free gas for months. I had grown up in Michigan and upon returning home, I received the answer as to why I had to leave Seattle and return to my home state. I was immediately set into motion with the thought in mind that the rest of my life was one of service. I began to focus on what that would be. I was satisfied with that answer and began to build my life around the gift of giving away my gifts to others. That is what Glenda looks like. If I had not listened to my intuitive message, I could have had a much more difficult time doing something that no longer served me. My life was to change and change drastically.

How fortunate I know that I am to have learned to stay open to messages that were coming not from my ego but from within. In the showing up process my answers were arriving through a series of events that would get me ready to be doing what I am today. And it takes a multitude of moments to have the answer. I know that because my ego is no longer able to trick me into thinking that my decisions do not include others.

So in my closet I put on those ruby reds and began my journey of the heart. I do not question myself in the present moment as to my life changing again because I now know it will. It always will. Great. Change is the birth of who I am in the moment.

Letting go is a much better state of mind than any other. It is the only time real peace and clarity can show up. The ego would love to rule the roost. The heart does not need to rule, it already has the answer. Giving it up is an affirmation of faith that creates affirmative action on our part; action that does not need to be analyzed or doubted.

As I write this, I find a smile on my face and a chuckle in my heart. I hear in my mind's eye a friend of mine saying, "Oh David! You are so Pollyanna!" I see him roll his eyes into the back of his head and then to complete the drama, a great big sigh. Am I insulted? Do I take this personally? Maybe I would have a few years ago but not today. I am happy, peaceful, joyous and free. I have a life that is of service. Everything I do, I seek from within, including the love I have for this longtime friend. I want him to have what I do. I would tell him that but why create a war? He gets the trip to Emerald City and then home if he wants it. And just like all of us, the opportunity will pop up in our lives several times. We will get nudged until we get it and even when we don't.

So on this incredible winding yellow brick road that we are on, we can go as far as we want to go. The tools and the guidance we need are sure to show up. If we are showing up to that next right thing, we will not be making a want list of material gains only. We will know in our hearts that we already have it all. Having it all is not having everything. Having it all means the all that we need to accomplish our mission here on planet earth. It comes with a breath. A breath of taking in the vapors that are good and a release of a breath for all that no longer serves us.

Having all of the knowledge that is available comes in increments of events and time. We will have the opportunity to see a great deal of life. Times of being shut down and unable to move because of grief or loss will happen to all of us. But we all will learn from this and conquer the fears that surround such events if we so choose. With each event—and especially the ones that are similar to others—the road gets easier. It is at this time that we may look back and wonder what took us so long to get it. Again, we need to remember it takes what it takes to get us where we are going and everything—everything is on time.

Fortunately for all of us, judgment is not in the mix of growth. We are allowed to make mistakes, just like we are allowed to have victories. Being harsh on myself or letting others play that role in our lives is the only hell we will everh experience. Personally, I sent the judges on to live with the shoulds and the what-ifs. It is a small community, but deadly if they are in my neighborhood. I would call this in my life the only epiphany I want to keep in the forefront of my thoughts. These folks are always trying to move back.

One important note that I must share about judgments is that I have been much harder on myself than the God of my understanding would ever be with me. It is good to let those judgments go, get back in the moment and know that this is an old movie that is no longer in circulation.

At the moment of realizing that we are ready to make our transition, many have been faced with regrets. They seem to be reviewing their lives with a sense of sadness because of some of the decisions they made. They may feel like the life they have lived has lacked what they had hoped for. But in the end, the present moment is still the key to not having self-judgment. The present moment in the end is knowing what we know, feeling what we feel, and accepting how far we have come. This in my estimation will promote a healthy cross over. We will be welcomed no matter what we want to lament over. Strength comes in knowing what you know. By knowing some of what you need to know early on and at the right time, you have a choice to move on to higher levels. A changed thought system produces those higher levels automatically. I personally have decided to have my heavenly experience here and now, and let it continue as I go on and ultimately leave the earth as I know it.

Surrender Dorothy! I'm Melting! I'm Melting!

If we don't surrender, we will be melting, melting away because we are not present to the next right thing to do. That word, *melting*, and the word *surrender*, can be ugly words or beautiful words. It all depends where we are with our pain. Even in a great deal of pain many of us are not willing to surrender. It can even take a lifetime to surrender or not surrender.

With an unhealthy ego involved in the letting go process of surrendering, we could stay in this insane thinking for a long time. One point is clear: we never get a chance at the right answer until we surrender. Accepting our moment of change, grief, or discord is the beginning of the end of misery.

I am sharing about surrender because I was never a good student when it came to this exercise. I needed a great deal of practice. Giving up a position or a feeling that no longer served me had become downright impossible. I held my position well. I did not listen and would not change, even with a fight. The lesson kept showing up until I finally showed up to surrender. I was finally starting to get it. But the pain and the agony of not giving up my will for God's will was stifling. To then find out that God's will lived within me was a real eye-opener. I needed every lesson I had, and I am glad the lessons did not let up. They will not let up if you ask for the answer on how to surrender. That old saying "Be careful what you pray for" rang true for me.

When the day came where I felt as if I was melting away, I finally started getting what it meant to live in the present moment. I stopped looking at my past as if it was never going to go away, and I finally got the message that my future was not even here yet. What in the world had I been thinking? It became clear that true surrender was the only way I would ever close a door to open a window.

The light went on in my new thought process, showing up, in the moment when I realized that if I kept doing things the same way, I would get the same results. That, to me, is insanity. I had been in a twelve step program that called this out as insanity. Getting rid of an addiction is only the beginning of learning a new way of living. I wanted it. I was willing.

When I had a problem, I surely did not want anyone to know, especially if it had to do with addiction. My disease started slowly, and worked great wonders for awhile. I could hide, have sex, socialize, pretend, and show off a lot of courage. Thank you, alcohol, for bringing me out of my shell and relieving me of the past judgments and the depression I had carried ever since I was a child. The party ended with a death, and when the party was over the rebirthing began. I finally was seeing who I really am. I was waking up.

My childhood had produced a great deal of baggage and I wanted to hide the baggage and act as if I was okay. I was not. I had no mentoring or role models on how to live my life. I was clueless. Letting others know this truth was not at the top of my list of things to talk about in social settings. I was heavy with baggage that had been weighing me down for years. I had grown up in a family that had no formula of how to live. My parents had not been taught by their parents and were not able to teach their three children. Their story was not any better than mine. Teaching what you don't have is not possible.

Growing up as a Jehovah's Witness was a way of life that had little opportunity. It was a religion of fear and many nos. No Christmas, no birthdays, no holidays, no school functions, no recognizing the flag, no fellowship with anyone outside the religion. The list could go on an on but today I find that list unimportant. I have recognized that this religious sect has loosened up somewhat. But when I was growing up, my life was limited to their beliefs, their five meetings a week and a constant fear of 1975, which they had earmarked as the end of the world. Fear was constant. It is what it is, and I thank God I live a life of choices. I have no ill will. It took years to detoxify from this misinformation, but I have been successful in finding oneness in us all.

Being raised in a religion that predicted the end of the world and loss of life if one did not follow their teachings was, I admit, very unnerving. My parents were entrenched in these beliefs. My mother because of my father. My father, after getting us involved in five meetings a week, field service, and other commitments, declined to attend anymore. He had started to judge, compare, and complain about the people that attended the meetings. But in all honesty he was battling what today would be diagnosed as bipolar disorder, in addition to other forms of mental illness.

My two siblings and I lived within a family that was hiding, and we were taught to lie. Witnesses did not smoke but were allowed to drink in moderation. Both my parents smoked and we lived in a small Cape Cod-clad house that was white on the outside and blue with smoke on the inside. The moment that an unexpected car pulled in our driveway, the panic bell went off. The trained seals, meaning my brother and sister and me, had a job to do. Quickly we hid all the ashtrays, spraying the entire home as fast as we could to make sure that the Jehovah's Witness showing up unexpectedly would not find out that my parents smoked. My parents were moving as fast as we were. If caught they would be "dis-fellowshipped," and that meant dying at Armageddon. Everything had to be discarded and hidden that would indicate that they smoked. It was total bedlam. Even though we were living in a mad house of verbal and physical abuse, as children we were not prepared to offer up our parents to the guillotine at the Kingdom Hall. The funniest part of this story in my life today is that no matter how many air fresheners one sprays or cigarettes one removes, the smell of cigarette smoke does not go away. The blue cloud lingers and the smell is stale and nasty. I guess if the Witnesses knew, they ignored my parents breach of contract.

We had been taught from early life that we, as children, were to also hide the truth about our parents and what went on in our home. It was a home of fear and anger, beatings, and a great deal of verbal as well as physical abuse. My father was sick with his own life and did things to his family that were unbearable. Being the oldest, I did my best to take care of my mother and stay clear of my father. He was not my friend, and he did not fail to ridicule me on a regular basis. He did not like me. So why share this tidbit of my secret family? Because if you have been there or in a similar situation, it does not have to be a way of life for the rest or your life. We have choices, lessons, and help to become all that we are, even under circumstances that were unbearable. I learned a great deal from my family. Today I am filled with compassion and answers for others that are in that situation, or living as an adult with the memory of that past horror.

We are the products of our environment. We cannot help that. We are affected and we do need to heal. I wanted to break the cycle. I knew at a very young age that I had a lot of work to do if I was to survive my family of origin and break the cycle that had left me hanging in a world that was supposed to be mine to enjoy. I am sure today that my parents never intentionally abused themselves or their children, teaching them to lie. They were in their own survival mode. I left home at sixteen, finished high school. I tried going to college but just could not swing the expense on my own. College would come in my midlife.

I continued as a young adult, finding my own survival mode. I wanted to distance myself from my family of birth and so I did. Like many others with a need to distance hurt, I chose alcohol. I medicated myself with it until I no longer hurt, and it no longer worked. I was faced with many situations that I would be dealing with. Alcohol became one of those many situations, but I used this substance as long as I could to maneuver through a life that looked okay. I am thankful today that I had that substance. I am thankful today that I no longer need that substance.

In my late twenties I shared with my best friend that I knew I was going to die by the time I was forty. I told Mary that I kept getting the same message over and over. It was a subconscious thought that came out of the blue at the most unexpected times. I died at forty. On my fortieth birthday I found myself in a treatment center in the state of Washington, recovering from alcoholism. My death came swiftly after a great deal of suffering. I was beaten down and could no longer handle the hangovers. I was not showing up to work, and I was drinking in the morning. I could no longer sleep and my monkey mind was threatening me with suicide. My good friend Richard was the one I called for help that fateful morning of pacing up and down and chugging beer. He showed up and was not convinced I needed to go into a treatment program for the disease of alcoholism. I assured him that I needed to go, and he needed to take me. My office had planned a big party that day for my fortieth birthday. I would not be attending that party but I had another party to attend. The party of sobering up. It was ugly and raw, and I needed to be in a safe place while I let my body detoxify from the summer of heavy alcoholic drinking. But I somehow knew that this was my opportunity to be reborn and say goodbye to an old life. It was a welcome death. Granted, it felt like a breech birth. Nothing worked, nothing felt right and I was faced with who I was not. I was faced with who I had pretended to be all those years. I finally did a small surrender and found myself forced to change just one thing: everything!

People, places and things had to change. People that I had associated with needed to be let go. I had multiple issues to address, and I was stone sober and felt like the AA saying, "a hole in the donut." It was the beginning of the end of a way of living. I must admit that if I could have seen the future and what I would need to do to change, I most likely would never have chosen this new path. I understand to this day, what *one day at a time* means. It means to stay in the now. It means growing spiritually to a point that is far beyond the addiction that got me to that first surrender. I have realized that for all of us, it takes a wakeup call and alcohol was mine.

So in showing up to AA I had to surrender, and then I had to surrender to everything that I had done or known before. We cannot show up if we are not willing to surrender. Without this gift of surrender, we live in self-justification, self judgment, working resentments, poor mental and physical health and no liaison to spiritual gifts. A door cannot open for us until we surrender.

We get in a position, once we have surrendered, to finally show up totally unencumbered by our past, and to be willing to not make up our future. We find ourselves truly in the moment. We will have to learn how to stay there but just to feel that feeling in the moment is awesome. A quick sense of peace comes over us at first. It may be a fleeting moment but it tells us of things to come, like more peace.

As we start the journey to peace we get a great deal of practice. There will be a series of events that come to pass that we will learn how to react to differently. For example we may feel ambushed totally out of the blue. We are unaware, and there they are right in our face. Your heart starts pounding and your adrenalin is pumping. Do I medicate? Do I run? Do I learn not to react to someone else's bad day? If you have chosen answer number three, you get to be a flying monkey for a week just for the fun of it. I had many lessons in learning not to react, along with a few ambushes. I learned that someone else's bad day was not mine to own. In the event someone was going to try to steal my energy, I did have the power within to take a breath and not get caught in someone else's lessons. I had enough to deal with. I could choose not to take on an energy vampire too. So, grab Toto and go for a nice long walk. Get out of that energy with grace and dignity. It's not your meltdown.

Choose Your Champions!

When we find ourselves—and we all do—in a time of indecision, there are three things we can do to find our way out. Shutting down the thinker, which is the ego in disguise, listening to our heart, and sending out the truth of who we are with affirmative declarations. I am the mind of God. The mind of God lives in everything I see, feel and touch. God is my cause to live and effect is the manifestation and the outcome.

Can you imagine trying to explain to someone that you know or love that you think this way? Can you hope for understanding from friends and family that are not on this enlightened path yet? This is the time you choose your champions. These are the people that know you live with the mind of God and that they too are connected to the identical energy. These champions stand next to you without judgment and without comment on what-ifs or what you should do. Instead they are lovingly supportive of your next right decision. They may have their own story that might fit into your indecision, and they may have a suggestion. Do they have the answer or do you?

These champions always show up at the right time and in varied form. An author, a chance meeting in the grocery store, a call from an old friend or a close friend that was just thinking about you. They are so willing to listen without judgment. They honor you by listening and they stay with you in the now, giving you full attention.

Yet there are slips for all of us, even the enlightened ones as we come face to face with a fearful decision that we have to make. We may find ourselves asking for advice and help about what to do? Almost as if we are closing our car door with the locks down and the keys still in the ignition, we get a sense of panic. There is no turning back. They are now going to tell me what I need to do. And why did I ever ask them to do so? Why did I do this and put myself through the misery of a person giving me advice about something they know so little about? This, in my world, is called *I-asked-for-it-karma*. These are not your champions but they are your lessons. The truth that you are seeking always lives within you.

In the end, someone is giving you advice. The rises in blood pressure, the resentments that set in and the self-judgment, all become a huge sinkhole.

Remembering the lesson will help us in the next encounter of needing a champion to show up. We will not be empowering everyone we see with what we think a problem is. We will not be on the phone, doing emails, texting, or on Facebook telling the world about something we have the ability to already know within us. The champions do show up at the perfect time. It will not come in the disguise of an overzealous ego. But the champion will be easily recognized because of the peace, love, and compassion that are energetically in front of you.

In my personal journey, when I was willing, my champions were there for me. I love my champions. They know that I know that I know. And their egos needs no massaging to feel as if they are in control of my destiny. They may suggest but usually they suggest by nudging me into what they know I already know. They sit tight and are attentive. They can hear whatever I have to say without comment. My champions listen, watch, and allow me to show up to the next right thing in my life. May I say that as I write this, I am feeling an overwhelming amount of gratitude? I know that I have to play my part too, but to be able to recognize my champions is incredibly freeing.

We all are either rebirthing or not. Change is a certainty but what is important is how we react to change and if we are willing to rebirth and go to the next level or step. To have a champion in a rebirthing state is the midwife to completion. Maybe all we can do is pick up where we left off, and that is okay too. There will be champions all around that are your angels of transformation. All we have to do is faithfully believe.

Some will say that failure is not an option. True. It is the opportunity. Failure has to happen, in some instances, to understand the value of the journey to success. Just knowing how extravagantly loved I am by the universe and knowing that no one else is left out, is a calming intuitive sense of what oneness really is. So if we end up judging ourselves in a harsh manner, so be it! But to know how totally unnecessary it is, will move us to our next adventure of a journey that we find so fortunate to be on.

Of course the humor of the human condition has not gone unnoticed by me. If I want to have a laugh, I just take a look at me. I am a laugh and a half. When having a day that is challenging I often say out loud, "I am schizophrenic and so am I." Then I check my zipper.

The real message that I would like to leave myself and the reader with, is that we are all champions for each other. Our answers live within us, and when we need each other to be nudged to the next level, let's just show up for ourselves and our friends. Let us be great listeners. Our friends and families need us, as does the unexpected person that shows up in our life and needs some help. We are here together because we are supposed to be together. To me that means we are living universally as one mind and one energy, and we all have the mind of God with all of the answers we will ever need. Be the champion you are looking for! Just show up! You gotta do it anyway.

Expose the Man behind the Curtain

Hello Mr. Ego. Let's really take some time to understand who you are. We touched on your involvement in our lives, and why you are not really or friend. So you are the one that is doing the light show, pulling all the levers, and sending out smoke and mirrors to throw me off. You make it look so real! Now to mention the fear that keeps me stuck from pulling that curtain back to expose you as an impostor. There comes a time when we all want to rip down that curtain and see who is really back there. We want to but we are also afraid. The what-ifs are present, and then there are the shoulds hanging on every untrue thought and word.

The ego has tried to convince us that the wizard has the answers to the past, and can project the future. In the wizard's point of view there is no present moment. The wizard keeps us way too tied up in staying out of the moment. When you are dealing with the ego and the wizard, it can be too fearful to look directly at the wizard in the wake of the present moment. But we will always have the choice. We can take the chance to take a look and address the present moment, or take a lifetime of looking and choosing not to. Without intention, action, trust and faith, we will never get rid of the wizard and all his smoke and mirrors.

In the beginning, we start our journey with the acceptance of a trusting child. We feel and are in the moment. But after our exposure to life on life's terms, we lose our freedom to the moment and start hearing the fears of others in regards to what will happen and what has happened. As children we know what we need in the moment and how to scream to get it. As an adult we may scream and get it, but there is no peace in what we get. We are always screaming out of fear of what could be because of what was.

In a near to normal setting, having parents who are in tune to raising their children with love, devotion, discipline, and mantras that express the best of who we are is an amazing start. These children will still have their life lessons but probably not as brutal as the children that did not have this kind of a healthy start. There are parents who missed the healthy starts themselves and have not learned how to parent. But over time and through conscious investigation, the cycle of unhealthy living over generations can be—and for many has been—broken. The awareness of an unhealthy cycle is the first step to taking the quantum leap toward stopping it. I know this because I had to take that leap.

With mental illness in my family, I had to learn early on how to dodge my father and protect my mother. My mother was twenty-one-years-old when she married my thirty-two-year-old father. Because of her own low self-esteem, she thought that this older man who worked and gave her attention was a miracle for her. But, as most people like my mother, she did not see the early warning signs of the problems that my father had. She was in the bliss of a new marriage and her future thinking was in full force with the thought of security and a house full of children. And for the twenty-three years that she stuck it out, she rarely ever saw a present moment. Instead she was always planning how to please or dodge my abusive father. I was her champion as the oldest child. I hurt for her, loved her, and tried my best to protect her. However, her loyalty was not with me but with my father. He was the feared one in our household. I feared him too. Not only did he physically abuse my mother, brother, sister, and me, but he verbally demoralized us, which was much worse. In my mother's fantasy world of thinking she could fix him by being everything to him and taking the abuse, she finally realized that it was impossible. It took twenty-three years to figure out that her marriage had to terminate, and it was not until the final chapter of abuse and abandonment that she finally heard the still, small voice inside her with a very direct answer-command. She was now ready to take the fearless action she would need to take.

With the death of my brother at nineteen, my father totally lost his sense of reality and attempted suicide. He was living with a mentality of revenge to find the boy that had been driving the car that killed my brother. It had been an accident, but not in his eyes. The fact that my brother was emotionally unstable, in trouble with the law, and drag racing on a stretch of expressway with his pregnant girlfriend in the car did not even cross his mind as he continued to search and harm this young man. He was obsessed with yet another drama that was playing out in his life. The pills and alcohol were flowing freely and his temper raging.

The next two years with my father were turbulent and unnerving until I got him institutionalized so that he would not harm himself or others. To his brother's dismay, because of the mark of mental illness that would be on the family name, I took the advice of the local police department after his third attempt to commit suicide and had him committed to a safe place. I wanted him to get the help he needed.

Why would I share this? I have to because, for me, it was the beginning of taking a good look at who this man was that I resented. It was the beginning of understanding that what he had done to me had previously been done to him. I was getting an opportunity to start a new way of thinking, and this would include a forgiveness step. This man and his true soul were something I had rarely seen, if ever. It took years for me to finally see who he was.

He eventually did commit suicide, and that is when he and I finally started healing. He came to me in a dream. I was building him a rock garden on Lake Michigan because he loved rock gardens. He walked down a set of steps and kneeled next to me and said, "Dave, I am sorry." I said to him, "I understand Dad and know everything for you will be okay." I have not heard from him since. I know he is safe in a classroom with people that love him, and he is finally getting a chance for the love he seemed to never have in his earthly life. He could not have the love he wanted because he had been so wounded he had nothing to give. I was relieved after this dream and knew that he would not haunt me or my thoughts any longer. The healing had begun for both of us. Today I know that the mind of God is in all of us; I am able to look at him long after he finally did commit suicide, and forgive myself for hating him and forgive him for hating himself so much that he abused everything in sight. His abuse to my family, neighbors, and fellow workers, was only enhanced by alcohol and prescription drugs. This was a toxic mix for a mentally ill, bipolar person. Today I realize he was trying to find a quick fix. His ending was horrific and he left this earth with five people at his funeral. The bartender, the waitress, and two patrons from where he sat every day to tell his wounded story of the family that deserted him. I was there along with my aunt, my mother and my sister, soberly sitting through my father's last stand.

The time for me to look more closely at my father came later. I discovered compassion for him and embraced the fact that his life was not mine. I had to love him enough to let him go. I had to love myself enough to make sure I let him go. I had learned later of his rocky start. Being the youngest of three boys, he had not been a surprise pregnancy for my grandmother. Without nurturing and unconditional love from his own father, he grew up fearful and feeling rejected. The physical and verbal abuse he received was passed on to his own family. The gene for alcohol addiction ran rampant on both sides of my family of birth. The story was over for me. I let go and healed. I broke the cycle.

As a child and young adult, I hid in a cocoon never knowing that a butterfly could emerge under the right circumstances. I learned in the cocoon how to be safe. I read my books. I asked questions. I used alcohol to come out of the cocoon occasionally so that I could dance, laugh, and be what I thought was a normal guy. But my wings never dried and back I had to go. My childhood graduated into adulthood with very few life skills. I had witnessed three family generations that had not healed. People that knew me in my early youth and knew my family gave me little hope to escape what appeared to be my destiny.

As I emerged and found my groove, I also found and recognized the many gifts that I had come into this life with. I began to use them. I was showing up, and it was fantastic. But little did I know that I had much to learn in the process of showing up. I had to learn the truth about what it took to do the next right thing. It was a process.

I was forty years old when I finally ripped down the curtain. At the time I thought that it might be easier to die. But as I explained earlier on in this book, it takes what it takes to catch our attention. Today I am a grateful guy that needed to be beaten down so that I would finally surrender an old way of life for a new way of living.

I became willing and accepted that I would do whatever it takes to find out who I really was. In doing so, I let go of the past in increments of time as I healed. I stopped projecting a future that I had no clue about in terms of how it would evolve. I just had a lot of thoughts. Some of those thoughts were good but they were not healing thoughts of intention, trust, and faith that would result in a manifestation in my best interest. No, I was caught for a while in a movie I made up. With my obsessive-compulsive nature, I used this negative to become a positive. I choose what was best for me to be obsessive and compulsive about. The choices were good and kept me on track.

Showing up became a huge plus! Forgiving myself and others was the key. This all worked as long as I stayed in the moment.

I was fortunate in so many ways and when I saw my Dad's soul for the first time, it was an awesome experience. I embraced his pain and felt true compassion. I forgave him for what I was holding him accountable for. I had reacted, and now I was learning to delete those feelings he had unintentionally left with me. I loved him for all that he was and all that he could have been on this planet. I was cleansing, and what a relief for my own soul! I had changed my thinking, and lo and behold, doors were opening for me. The air was fresh. I was fresh. I was feeling my wings finally drying.

It was at this transformational moment that I gave myself permission and encouragement to take the rest of my journey, one day at a time. I had always been in flight. I stopped running from the man behind the curtain. I was no longer afraid, and worry was becoming an old way of being.

So this particular part of my message can relate to many people with varied circumstances. However, I know it is directly pointed at those of us who are tired of not being on the side of healing. This message is for those who may be stuck but could, if they choose, pick up where they left off.

What a gift to know that our dreams are who we are, and that they can come to us by the willingness to change our thoughts, followed by action and, most of all, faith. Turning my life over to the care of the universal mind of God was the most courageous and fearless step I ever took. This is a step that is not for a few but for all. We live in a oneness that once recognized, breaks open the cocoon that releases us to become magnificent butterflies.

Be the Star of Your Own Show!

What a final chapter this will be. Yes, it is all about you, and who doesn't like that? You are the main character in your show and you even get to produce and direct the adventure series from beginning to end. You decide if you are going to do drama, adventure, or both. Your story, like mine, can be open-ended or about past experiences. Experiences that you have not yet let go of can tell the same story over and over again. It is great to know we have the choice. Of course you will be getting the same results if your story is not going to change. You could make your story be an adventurous book that transforms from drama to a new story. Your readership will increase and you will be attracting new and wonderful adventures into your life. A rags-to-riches story always is a best-seller and is sure to be a movie that everyone will love to watch. Choose your story with intention, believe it and let it happen!

If you are not ready to tell your story of authenticity and transparency, you will still be telling a story. It will be the story of resentments, judging others, money laundering, self-loathing, sickness, and ultimate death. There may be even a murder or two in one of the concluding chapters. Or maybe the murder is your own suicide, of your old way of thinking. Addiction could be a chapter in your life. The way you acted out and the way you lost your way until you surrendered. Or did you?

You will find there are many lifetimes and many shows that can take place in a lifetime. As you grow, the plot and the show will change. You will find that as you grow, you change. Then you are able to rebirth as many times as you want. What started out as dark and depressing with a head full of characters that are trying to run the show, will eventually, without notice, change into an enlightened moment of recognition that you have the power to change your world.

All those years of listening to the many voices of doom and gloom are on the chopping block. Your illusive life is disappearing and the real deal is starting to show up. You have an option of showing up to this new way as soon as you refuse to give power to the fear in your life. And there it is, the spotlight! You are in the ring of light, and the performance of a lifetime begins.

The audience is attentive as you are playing to a like-minded group of souls that you have been attracting with this new way of playing our authentic part. It is truly a Rolaids moment: relief!

By taking the time of recognizing the now, you recognize that everything in your past can be changed. If the past rears its head, it is only a reference point for what works and what does not. Your future is promised as your now is so right-on that you are cocreating a future with God that will be spot on.

Life will still have its challenges, because there is one thing that is always a part of your life, and as it should be: change. But with what you have learned about cause and effect, change is as natural to us as a trip to the grocery store. You are learning that your thinking dictates the changes you will experience, as well as the ultimate outcomes. You accept change and you embrace the results. To surrender in this moment of change is the bravest act of strength you could ever take!

If you become a Rip Van Winkle temporarily and fall asleep on the job, you are not judged by anyone but yourself. That is to say that your judgments are the only ones that count, good or bad. Part of the surrender is letting go of anyone that would make the mistake of judging you. Remember, everyone secretly wants to be the star of their own show, and sometimes by judging someone else they feel as if they are in the spotlight. They are, but the bulb is burning out quickly, and darkness overtakes the stage until a new thought of life brings the brilliance back.

Your show is all about showing up, and you get to decide if you want to show up to the ego or the heart in your quest to show up to the next right thing. The summary of your life, as well as this book, is all about taking the information you have been given and not turning back. It is about making a decision to alter an old way of thinking to receive a new way of doing. You are your own destiny and are so connected to the vapors of the energized universe that if you choose to start listening with intention and take action, you will be skyrocketed into the best show on earth. You will be the star, and all who watch your show will want to have a piece of the action. You will intuitively know that everyone already has a piece of the action. You will discover oneness, and it will be time to welcome in everyone and eliminate any thought of separation.

Your show will need to be written in the moment. It will have a beginning and middle and an end. But the most important value to your show will be the now that you have claimed to write into your story. With a mistake or two along the way, you can also throw the plot into a rewrite, knowing that it is okay to make a mistake. Mistakes have now become your opportunity to successful living. You are entrenched in every moment and enjoying the ride. You will have the tools to show up to the next right thing every day so that you can keep writing your script.

You live in a universe that knows only life, and as the seasons change so do you.

Rebirthing gives us opportunity to reach a higher level of what some call the Christ or Buddha consciousness. At this level of consciousness you receive the understanding of oneness. You find unconditional love for all people, and you no longer embrace anything that is separate. You intuitively know that you and everyone else are part of the same God, the same universe. This is not in any way discrediting the God of your understanding. Moreover it is acknowledging that in all teachings that are of the good, we will find the same teaching of oneness. Getting to this point is not a race, and as much time as is needed can be taken.

Death is not an option. Rebirth is the reality. We all have the gift of time.

Finding your peace and hope in enlightenment is constant and is an ever-unfolding process. With peace, a creative change is clearly visible to you and those who have joined your journey. You find yourself loving extravagantly in the now. What a formula to embrace a successful sacred contract. You finally find out exactly why you are here and what you have been gifted to do. The best part of finding out is the fun, peace and prosperity you will have.

So just like Dorothy on her quest to get home, you too will find the balloon that will carry you back to your Kansas. You can now stay in the homeland of your heart and continue on a journey of amazement and wonder, without the fear of the man behind the curtain.

As you become present to your journey I can only suggest that you tap into your intuitive self, the one that meets you in the moment with your higher self to reveal all the answers. It is the first-class journey of this lifetime. You are here to go first class, but you will first have to know that you were on the list for that kind of living. Everyone is on that list, and if your fellow travelers have not yet discovered this, you are here to share this treasure of information.

Now it becomes time to do what we humans do. You want to rate your own performance. If you are doing your best and you know it, you can give yourself a 4.0. Then there are those days when you are trying to do your best, but it just does not feel as if you got there. But if you look back and you note that you were doing the best you could under the circumstances you were faced with, it would be good of you to not give yourself a 2.8. Your best, under all conditions, will always be a 4.0 day.

You can wait for a heaven that is far off, or you can have your heaven today. Thank God for the wizards, the scarecrows, the lions and the witches. And thank God for all the Auntie Ems that show up right when you need them on your journey to get home and stay home.

With the continued practice of letting go, you learn how to receive a formula for a great life, full of promise, and all the gifts you had ever hoped for.

I hope that this book has nudged you toward a journey of showing up to your life. I do not have your answers but I am absolutely positive you do. I have my answers, and I know that I am not the only lucky one. Try meditation and the quieting of the mind in any fashion that works for you personally. Take a walk in a natural setting, cross your legs, stand upside down, listen to music—do whatever it takes to get to a quiet, meditative moment. There is no right or wrong way. Do whatever works. Your higher self—the God of your understanding—lives within you. It will be so reassuring to finally know that you know that you know that you know.

It's *your* turn! Go ahead! Slip on those gender-neutral ruby reds and take the journey that only *you* can take! It's been waiting for you. Just *show up*! Be the star you are.

Namaste.

Author's Note

I hope you enjoyed *Just Show Up* as much as I enjoyed sharing it with you. Watch for my next book, *Emotional Rags to Spiritual Riches*, coming in 2014.

Printed in the United States
by Baker & Taylor Publisher Services